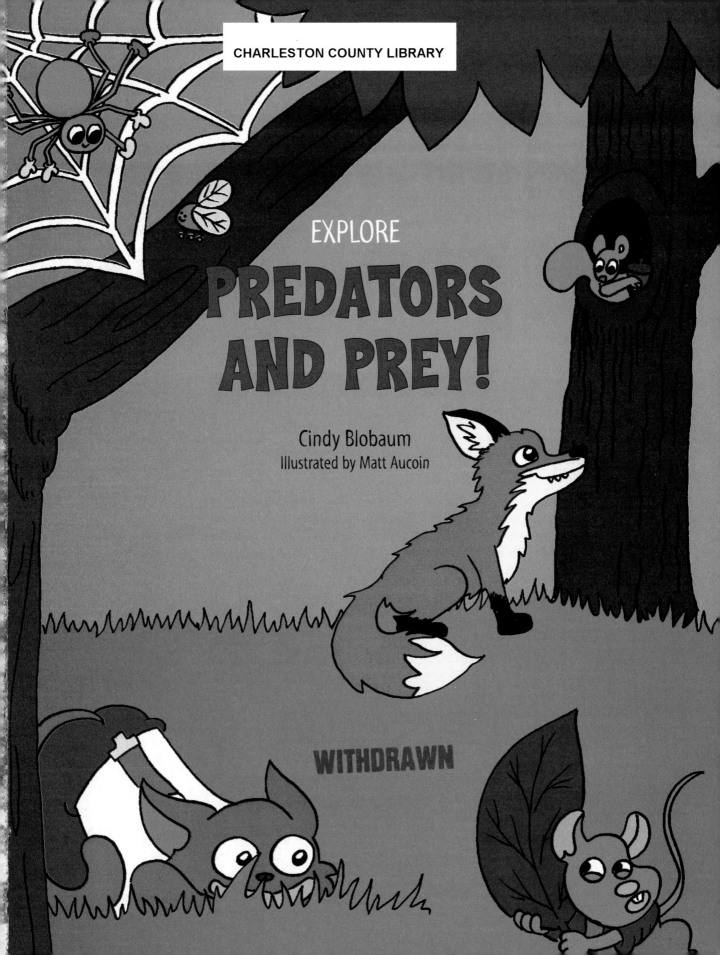

EXPLORE

PREDATORS AND PREY!

Cindy Blobaum

Illustrated by Matt Aucoin

Recent science titles in the **Explore Your World!** Series

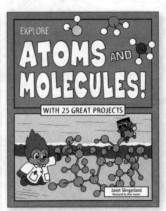
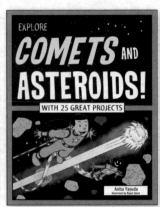

Check out more titles at www.nomadpress.net

Nomad Press
A division of Nomad Communications
10 9 8 7 6 5 4 3 2 1

This book was manufactured by Marquis Book Printing,
Montmagny, Québec, Canada
December 2016, Job #125545

ISBN Softcover: 978-1-61930-460-4
ISBN Hardcover: 978-1-61930-456-7

Educational Consultant, Marla Conn

Questions regarding the ordering of this book should be addressed to
Nomad Press
2456 Christian St.
White River Junction, VT 05001
www.nomadpress.net

Printed in Canada.

THANK YOU

to naturalists Matt Crayne, Mike Krebill, and Karen Phelps for their ideas and support.

CONTENTS

Interested in primary sources? Look for this icon.
Use a smartphone or tablet app to scan the QR code and explore more!
You can find a list of URLs on the Resources page.

If the QR code doesn't work, try searching the Internet with
the Keyword Prompts to find other helpful sources.

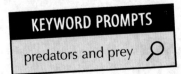

KEYWORD PROMPTS

predators and prey

Animals have always been predators and prey. This timeline covers human interactions, mainly in the United States, that have had significant impacts on predator and prey populations. Similar stories can be found in other nations around the world.

1909: Aldo Leopold, now described as the "Father of Wildlife Management," starts his first job after college with the U.S. Forest Service in the territories of Arizona and New Mexico.

32,000 BCE: Humans record their hunting activities with paintings on cave walls in Europe.

1907: Humans decide to remove all predators from the Kaibab Plateau in Arizona in order to protect the deer. By 1939, more than 8,000 predators have been killed. The deer population grows so large that the deer cannot find enough to eat.

4000 BCE: Egyptians record hunting and fishing activities with paintings on tomb walls.

2000 BCE: Native nations in the American Southwest use reeds and other plants to create decoys to help them attract ducks and geese to hunt.

1364 CE: First recorded use of a gun.

MARCH 1, 1872: U.S. President Ulysses S. Grant signs a bill that creates the first national park in the United States, Yellowstone National Park.

SEPTEMBER 1, 1914: The last passenger pigeon dies. These birds become extinct due to over hunting by humans.

1926: The last wolf pack in Yellowstone National Park is killed.

DECEMBER 28, 1973: U.S. President Richard Nixon signs the Endangered Species Act into law. This law protects any animal or plant in the United States that is in danger of becoming extinct.

1995–1996: Thirty-one gray wolves from western Canada are relocated to Yellowstone National Park.

1974: The gray wolf is listed as an endangered species. Government agencies work to protect and restore wolf populations and habitats.

MAY 4, 2008: The status of the Yellowstone National Park gray wolves is changed from Endangered to Experimental: Non-Essential.

2009: The states of Montana and Idaho open a regulated hunting season on gray wolves.

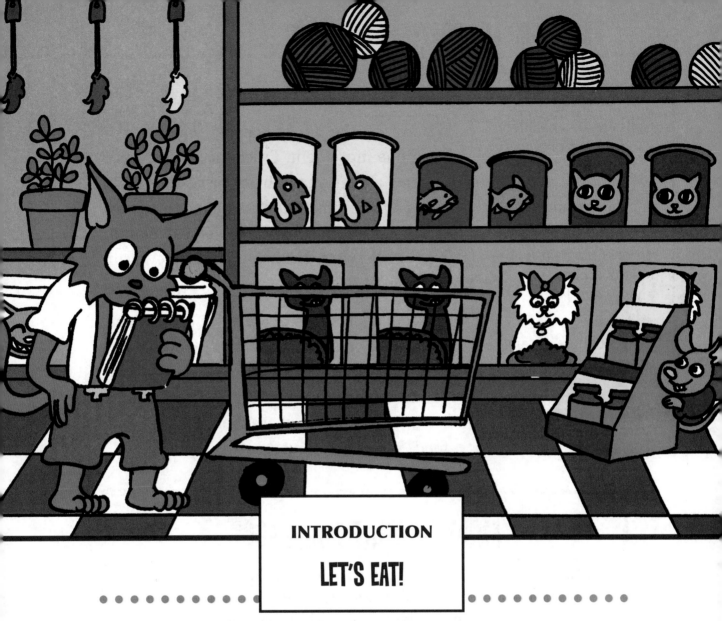

INTRODUCTION

LET'S EAT!

Every living thing, including you, needs energy to live and grow. Most plants get all of their energy from the sun. Most animals get all of their food by eating plants, other animals, or some of both.

What did you have for breakfast this morning? Did that food come from a plant or an animal? Foods such as apples, carrots, and oatmeal come from plants. Foods such as eggs, bacon, and sausage come from animals.

WORDS TO KNOW

energy: the ability or power to do things, to work.

1

WORDS TO KNOW

cell: the basic unit or part of a living thing. Cells are so small they can be seen only with a microscope. Billions of cells make up an animal or plant.

photosynthesis: the process plants use to convert the sun's energy into food.

organism: a living thing, such as a plant or animal.

Many of the foods we eat have more than one ingredient. Crackers, yogurt, and cookies are all made from more than one thing. Wild animals can't combine things to make their dinner. They either eat plants just as they are, animals just as they are, or some of each.

Eating seems like a pretty simple thing. But where does your food come from? Most people get their food from a grocery store, cafeteria, restaurant, or garden. If we didn't have those places, where would you go for food? What would you eat?

ANIMALS THAT MAKE FOOD

Plant cells use sunlight to make the energy the plant needs to grow. Plants do this in a process called photosynthesis. That's why trees and flowers don't need mouths! Scientists have discovered a few animals that have cells that can use sunlight to make food, including the sea slug and the spotted salamander. These animals use algae cells to transform sunlight into energy. Algae are simple organisms that are like plants but do not have roots and leaves. Other animals use electricity to make food!

PS

You can read about these animals and look at their pictures at this website.

KEYWORD PROMPTS

photosynthetic animals

For thousands of years, humans were hunters and gatherers. They had to find the plants and kill the animals that they ate. This is what most wild animals have to do all the time. And wild animals also have to make sure they aren't attacked and eaten by other animals.

WHY ARE FROGS SO HAPPY?

They eat whatever bugs them!

Predators are the animals that catch and eat other animals. The animals that predators eat are called prey.

There are predators and prey all around the world. Some even live near you! Do you ever see spiders in your house? Spiders are predators that catch and eat insects, which are their prey. An owl is a predator that hunts its prey of mice, rabbits, snakes, and other animals. A house cat is a predator that often catches small birds, moles, and rodents, such as mice.

There are also much bigger predators, such as wolves, mountain lions, polar bears, and some whales. Most of these larger predators live far away from humans.

adapt: how a plant or animal changes during long periods of time to survive in new or different conditions.

survive: to stay alive.

tool: an object that helps get a job done.

WORDS TO KNOW

There might be millions of different kinds of prey, such as ants, worms, deer, moose, and seals. Some animals can be both predator and prey. For example, bullfrogs hunt and eat dragonflies, small fish, and even small ducklings. Bullfrogs are also hunted and eaten by snakes, fish, and hawks.

This book is about predators and prey. You will learn about how living things kill or try to avoid being killed and eaten. You will learn how both predators and prey have adapted to survive. Have fun testing some tools for trapping and tricking and building models to make you a better hunter or hider. You will practice skills for staying safe and learn how our wild world is in an ongoing balancing act that is always changing.

TINY PREDATORS

The world's smallest predators have only one cell! Warnowiids live in water and are smaller than the period at the end of this sentence. They hunt other single-celled animals using structures that look similar to tiny harpoons. Scientists have discovered that these tiny creatures have a structure in them that is very similar to the human eye! We don't know yet how the warnowiids use these.

PS You can see pictures and watch a video about warnowiids at this website.

KEYWORD PROMPTS

National Geographic warnowiid

GOOD SCIENCE PRACTICES

Every good scientist keeps a science journal! Do the activity on page 8 to make your own science journal. As you read through this book and do the activities, keep track of your observations in a scientific method worksheet, like the one shown here. Scientists use the scientific method to keep their experiments organized.

Step	Example
1. Question: What are we trying to find out? What problem are we trying to solve?	Are you predator or prey?
2. Research: What information is already known?	Books at the library say humans are predators because many people eat meat, even if most of it is from farms.
3. Hypothesis/Prediction: What do we think the answer will be?	I think we are predators.
4. Equipment: What supplies are we using?	Food tracking worksheet, science journal
5. Method: What procedure are we following?	Keep track of the food you eat for one week.
6. Results: What happened and why?	Do you eat any meat? If so, you are a predator. Can you think of any animal that eats humans if they can? If so, you know that humans can also be prey!

Each chapter of this book begins with a question to help guide your exploration of predators and prey. Keep the question in your mind as you read the chapter. At the end of each chapter, use your science journal to record your thoughts and answers.

 INVESTIGATE!

How does where you live affect what you eat?

PROJECT!

TOP THIS!

Do plants or animals provide most of the energy for other living things? It would take a lot of time to observe and record the feeding habits of every type of animal, but you can easily put your own eating habits to the test and make a personal food pyramid.

SUPPLIES

* journal and pencil
* ruler
* colored sticky notes or index cards—green, red, and yellow
* digital camera (optional)

1 Make a journal using the project on the next page. On the left side of a double page, write "What do I eat most, plants, animals, or combined foods?" as the question on the first scientific method worksheet in your journal.

2 Do some research. What type of food do your family members and friends think you eat the most? Record their thoughts in your research section.

3 Write your prediction in the hypothesis section. You don't have to agree with what others think! You are doing this experiment to find out.

4 Use the ruler and pencil to make four columns on a blank page. Label the top of the first column "When Eaten." Label the top of the second column "Food from Plants." Label the top of the third column "Food from Animals." Label the top of the fourth column "Food from Plants and Animals."

PROJECT!

5 For one day, write down EVERY food you eat, even if it is just one pretzel. Don't worry about your drinks. Choices for "When Eaten" might include breakfast, lunch, snack, dinner.

6 If a food comes from more than one group, divide it up. For example, if you eat a hamburger on a bun with cheese, pickles, ketchup, and mustard, make six entries. Hamburger goes in the animal column. The bun, pickles, ketchup, and mustard each come from one or more plants. Write each of these on its own line in the plant column. Cheese could come from a mix of plant and animal, so write it in the last column.

7 At the end of the day, write each item from column two (plant foods) on a separate green card. Write each item from column three (animal foods) on a separate red card. Write each item from column four (both) on a separate yellow card.

8 Count the number of cards of each color. Place the largest number of colored cards in a row. Place the next highest number of colored cards above these. Place the colored cards with the fewest number on top. Take a photo or sketch this pyramid in your journal. Write the answer to the question at the top.

TRY THIS! Keep your food journal for more than one day. Does it change the results? Compare your food pyramid with one made by a friend. How similar or different are they? You can look at a food energy pyramid of mostly fresh, single-ingredient foods at this website.

KEYWORD PROMPTS

basic nutrition Crossfit 🔍

PROJECT!

PREDATOR AND PREY JOURNAL

Good scientists keep track of many things. They write down the things they wonder about and the questions they ask. They record the steps they take in the scientific method. Create a special notebook to help you keep track of what you do and learn about predators and prey.

SUPPLIES

* 3 to 4 sheets of 11-by-17-inch paper
* hole punch
* 5 to 10 sheets lined paper
* pencil
* 3-ring binder
* art supplies

1 Fold the sheets of 11-by-17-inch paper in half with a hamburger fold. You will use these when you do activities comparing predators and prey. You can record your observations about each group on different sides and see the results next to each other.

2 Place a piece of lined paper so the holes are along the folded edge of the 11-by-17-inch paper. Use the hole punch to make three holes in the 11-by-17-inch paper pieces so they can be kept in your binder.

3 Place all the sheets in the binder. You will use these pages to record the steps of the scientific method and your thoughts about the questions in each chapter.

4 Decorate the cover and get ready to learn!

CHAPTER 1

HIDE AND SEEK!

All wild animals must find food, unless they are babies who are taken care of by their parents. Most animals try to hide as they are looking for food. Prey animals hide so that it is harder for predators to find and eat them. Predators hide so they can get closer to their prey before they attack. Both predator and prey animals try to hide their babies!

INVESTIGATE!

Sight, smell, hearing, touch, and taste are your five senses. Which sense do many humans rely on the most?

mammal: an animal such as a human, dog, or cat. Most mammals are born live, feed milk to their young, and usually have hair or fur covering most of their skin.

reptile: an animal covered with scales that crawls on its belly or on short legs. A snake, turtle, lizard, and alligator are all reptiles.

amphibian: an animal, such as a toad, frog, or salamander, that usually spends at least part of its life in water.

camouflage: colors or patterns that allow a plant or animal to blend in with its environment.

WORDS TO KNOW

Did You Know?

Baby mammals, most baby birds, and many baby insects are fed by their parents. But baby reptiles, amphibians, most fish, spiders, worms, and many other animals have to find their own food as soon as they are born.

LOOK WITH YOUR EYES

One way to hide is to look the same as the world around you. The use of colors and patterns to blend in with the surrounding area is called camouflage. Camouflage patterns include stripes, spots, blotches, and zigzags. Another way animals use camouflage is to have different colors on the back and belly.

In the snowy Arctic, white snowshoe hares blend in with the landscape. This makes it harder for the white Arctic foxes to find them. In the rainforest, green parrots match the green leaves. The bright green tree boas can't see and catch them.

colorblind: unable to see certain colors.

habitat: the natural area where a plant or animal lives.

WORDS TO KNOW

Both reef sharks and Samson fish are dark colored on their backs and light colored on their bellies. If you are looking down in the ocean, their color matches the darker water below. If you are looking up at them, the light color looks more like the sun. Many animals are also colorblind, which makes it easier for prey to hide from predators.

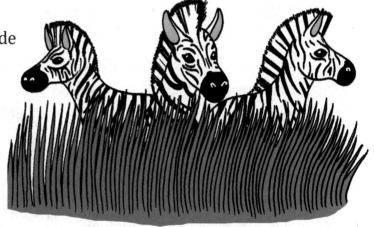

Another way animals hide is by having patterns that match their habitats. Tigers and zebras both have stripes, which help them hide. Tigers blend in with the jungle around them, and zebras can hide in tall grasses or blend in with large herds.

Other patterned animals include deer fawns and leopard cubs. Both of these baby animals have spots that help them blend in with the shadows and sun spots on the forest floor.

SMELL WITH YOUR NOSE

There is much more to hiding than just blending in and sitting still. Animals that are hiding don't want other animals to smell or hear them! How can an animal hide or seek with smell? How does an animal's smell help them avoid becoming prey?

Many predators and prey have very good senses of smell. Animals with long noses usually have better senses of smell than those with short noses. Dogs and their relatives, such as foxes, wolves, and coyotes, are better at detecting scents than cats, cougars, lions, and jaguars. The predators with the best senses of smell are bears, sharks, kiwis, and snakes.

Many baby animals are born without an odor. This helps to protect them. As long as their smelly parents aren't around, other animals might walk right past the babies.

Adult animals control their odor by grooming. They lick their smells right off. Some predators, such as wolves and coyotes, roll around in smelly things, including other animals' poop. Some scientists think the animals do this to hide their own smells. Human hunters have picked up on this idea and buy bottled smells of other animals to hide their own smells!

HEAR WITH YOUR EARS

Another important sense for animals is hearing. Many animals have ears that can move to follow sounds. Have you ever watched a dog's ears when they're listening carefully to something? Which way do they point?

downwind: to have an object between you and the direction of the wind.

WORDS TO KNOW

TRY IT!

On a windy day, wet one finger and raise it above your head. The side of the finger that cools first is the direction the wind is coming from. If you were a predator, you would want to be on the opposite, or warmer side of the finger. That side is downwind. Animals can use their whiskers to tell which direction the wind is blowing.

Some owls have ears at different positions on their heads. Sound reaches the lower ear faster than the higher ear, making it easier for the owl to know where the sound is coming from. An owl's sense of hearing is so good that it can catch its prey without even seeing it!

Animals try to move silently so they won't be heard by their predators or prey. They walk slowly, avoid crunchy leaves, and some burrow under snow. Owls have fringed feathers that help them fly without making a sound. They can sneak up on their prey and have a delicious dinner.

? CONSIDER AND DISCUSS

It's time to consider and discuss: Sight, smell, hearing, touch, and taste are your five senses. Which sense do many humans rely on the most?

CAMOUFLAGE COLORS AND PATTERNS

Many animals use colors or patterns or both to help them camouflage. Try your hand at designing an animal's coat to help it hide where you are!

Caution: Do not eat the colored crackers. Make sure to dispose of them where younger children or animals cannot get them.

1 On one page in your journal, write this question: Which type of coloring will best camouflage an animal where I live? Be sure to include your hypothesis.

2 Separate the crackers into three groups of equal numbers.

3 Keep one group of crackers plain. Color one group of crackers with single colors on each side. Decorate the third group of crackers with patterns, such as stripes, dots, and splotches in multiple colors.

Did You Know?

Many people pick up baby animals when they don't see a parent animal around. Usually, the parent is not far away or is looking for food. The parent might be staying away from the baby so predators don't smell it. You will help keep the baby animal safer by keeping away!

4 Toss the plain group onto a carpeted floor or yard outside. Start the timer. Pick up one at a time and place them in a line as you find each one. Time how long it takes to recover all the crackers. Record your results. Put the crackers to the side.

5 Toss the second group onto the same carpeted floor or outdoor yard area. Start the timer. Again, pick one up at a time and place in a line. Record the time it takes to recover all the crackers.

6 Toss the patterned group onto the same area and follow the same instructions. Compare your results.

7 On the next page in your journal, create what you think would be the ideal camouflage for an animal in your area!

THINK ABOUT IT: Do you think the results would be the same on a different floor or area of the yard? How could you test it?

PROJECT!

WATERPROOF WIND SOCK

Predators and prey are always paying attention to which way the wind is blowing. Moving wind carries the smells of other animals. Which way is downwind? Make this waterproof wind sock and find out!

SUPPLIES

* plastic drink bottle
* scissors
* hole punch
* string or yarn
* 2 to 3 colored plastic bags
* science journal and pencil
* compass

1 Use the scissors to cut a 2-inch-wide ring out of the drink bottle. Punch holes on opposite sides of the ring.

2 Cut a piece of string at least 4 feet long. Tie one end of the string in each hole.

3 Cut the plastic bags into long strips, about 1 inch wide. Fold each plastic strip in half.

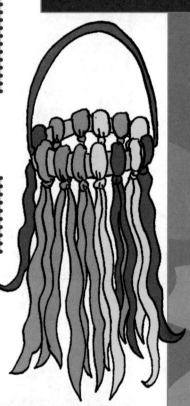

4 Push the folded end of one strip up through the middle of the bottle ring. Wrap the two loose ends on the other side of the ring and through the loop made by folded end. Pull tight. Repeat with the other plastic strips.

5 Hang your windsock on a branch or hook outside. Wind direction is the direction the wind is coming from. Line up a compass or direction app on a smartphone with the ring side of your wind sock to determine the wind direction.

6 Label a page in your journal: Wind Direction. Record the date and wind direction each day for two weeks. You can organize your data in a table like the one shown below. Does the wind blow from one direction more often than from the others?

Date	Wind Direction
Sunday, Week 1	
Monday, Week 1	
Tuesday, Week 1	
Wednesday, Week 1	
Thursday, Week 1	
Friday, Week 1	
Saturday, Week 1	
Sunday, Week 2	
Monday, Week 2	
Tuesday, Week 2	
Wednesday, Week 2	
Thursday, Week 2	
Friday, Week 2	
Saturday, Week 2	

TRY THIS! Wind socks can show direction, and they can also show speed. Read how you can use the wind sock to judge wind speed with the Beaufort wind scale.

KEYWORD PROMPTS

Beaufort wind scale 🔍

SCENTS SENSE

Hunters often use beagles to track rabbits and other animals. It is harder for the beagles to smell the rabbits on very cold or dry days. Can your nose detect odors on different objects at different temperatures?

1 Label a page in your journal "Scents Sense." Follow the scientific method and record your question, research, and hypothesis. Copy this chart to record your findings.

	Hot	Room Temperature	Cold
Rock			
Wood			
Cloth			

2 Make a code for each temperature. For example, a star for hot, a line for room temperature, and a circle for cold. Write the code in your chart and make one symbol on each solid item. So one rock will have a star, one rock will have a line and one rock will have a circle.

3 Dab a small amount of the smell on each item. Put the rock, wood, and cloth piece to be chilled in a plastic tub in a freezer.

4 Put the rock, wood, and cloth piece to be heated in a plastic tub in a closed vehicle in the sun on a sunny day.

5 Put the rock, wood, and cloth piece to stay at room temperature in a plastic tub on a table or counter. Keep the pieces in their places for at least two hours.

HOW DOES A LEOPARD CHANGE ITS SPOTS?

When it gets tired of one spot, it just moves to another!

6 When the time is up, pick up the rock that was kept at room temperature and put it under your nose. Can you smell the scent? Record your findings in your journal.

7 Before you try the next item, put your nose next to your arm and smell. This will reset your smell sensor before you try the next item. Smell your skin between each test!

8 Continue testing and recording your results for each item at room temperature, the freezer, and the warming zone.

9 Does your nose work better on warm or cold items? Does it work better on some items than others, no matter what the temperature is?

TRY THIS! If you see an animal with its lips curled up and mouth open, it might not be trying to bite, but to smell using their mouth! This is called flehmen's response. Try it by curling your lips back, opening your mouth, and breathing in through your mouth. Do you notice any difference?

EAR TRUMPET

The shape of an owl's face is similar to a satellite dish. This shape helps move sound toward the ear openings. Saw whet owls have one ear higher on their head and the other ear lower. What difference do those two adaptations make? Hear for yourself!

SUPPLIES

* science journal and pencil
* 2 sheets of copy paper
* tape
* chair
* friend
* blindfold
* 2 wooden pencils

1 Label a page in your journal: "Hearing Tap Test." Copy this chart in your journal.

Tap location	Got it with ears	Missed it with ears	Got it with tubes	Missed it with tubes
Over head				
In front of head				
Behind head				
Above head to the right				
Below seat to the right				
Above head to the left				
Below seat to the left				

WORDS TO KNOW

adaptation: a body part or behavior that has developed to do a specific job for an animal or plant.

2 Roll each sheet of paper into a cone shape. There should be a small hole at one end and a wide opening at the other end of each ear trumpet. Use tape to hold the cone shape in place.

3 Put the chair in an open area so you can walk all the way around it. The person being tested, or the subject, sits in the chair and puts on the blindfold.

4 Standing to the side, the tester holds the pencils about 8 to 12 inches away from the subject and taps them together quickly a few times. The subject points to where they think the sound is coming from. The tester moves the pencils to a new place and taps again. Record all the results in the chart.

5 Repeat the test, this time letting the subject use the cones. The small end of each cone should be placed close to, but not in the ears. The cones can be held straight out from the head, with one pointed up and the other down, or even one pointed to the front and one pointed to the back. Record the results.

6 Switch places and repeat the tests. Compare results. Did having tubes help or hurt your hearing?

TRY THIS! Make the ear trumpet in various sizes and shapes. Does it make a difference if the trumpet has a wide horn versus a narrow horn? Does the type of paper make a difference?

CHAPTER 2

TOOLS OF THE TRADE

The main job of every animal is to stay alive long enough to have babies. To do this, every type of animal needs a body and behaviors that help it. If an animal is a predator, it needs a body and behaviors that help it catch and eat other animals. Many predators have sharp teeth for biting and strong muscles for moving very fast.

If an animal is a prey, it needs a body and behaviors that help it find food and get away from predators. Many prey animals are skilled at evading or fooling predators. The body parts and behaviors that help an animal survive are called adaptations. Inside and out, from head to toe, each animal is a collection of adaptations.

 INVESTIGATE!

What tools set humans apart from other predators?

ADAPTING TO THE WORLD

Animals can't choose which adaptations they want to have to help them survive. A rabbit can't decide that it wants long, moveable ears and then go to the store and buy them! Adaptations become part of an animal's body during hundreds and thousands of years of evolution.

A long time ago, rabbits with longer ears had a better chance of surviving than those with shorter ears. When they had babies, the babies that had longer ears had a better chance of surviving, too. After many, many generations, most rabbits had longer ears.

WORDS TO KNOW

evade: to escape or avoid getting caught.

evolution: changing gradually during many years.

generation: a group born and living at about the same time.

stalk: to quietly follow prey.

inherit: to acquire something from a parent or grandparent.

> **Did You Know?**
> The three-toed sloth acts differently than many predators. It doesn't search, stalk, and chase its prey. When a lizard or bird happens to crawl across its unmoving body, the sloth grabs and eats it!

For each type of animal, the ones that have the bodies that work the best are the most likely to live to have babies. Their babies inherit those adaptations.

HUMAN VS. ANIMAL

Humans have adaptations, too! Our adaptations include our five senses—sight, hearing, smell, touch, and taste. Animals have these tools, too, but they sometimes work differently.

nocturnal: to be active at night.

echolocation: to find an object by making sounds, then hearing how the sounds bounce back to your ears.

WORDS ᴛᴏ KNOW

Think about your eyes. The eyes on your head face forward. This lets you be a good judge of speed and distance. Most predators, including owls and cougars, have forward-facing eyes.

However, you can't see very far on either side. This lets other animals easily sneak up on you. Prey animals, such as dragonflies and squirrels, have eyes on the sides of their heads. They can see all the way around, so nothing can sneak up on them! There's a rhyme to help you remember: Eyes in front, likes to hunt. Eyes on side, likes to hide.

You use your ears to hear, but your sense of hearing is different from that of dolphins and bats. These predators use a technique called echolocation. They send out high-pitched clicking sounds that bounce off the prey and back to the predator. These echoes help the predators find the moving prey.

Did You Know?

Animals with bigger eyes are usually nocturnal. Many animals with small eyes live underground or in caves.

ELECTRICAL SENSE

Fish, sharks, and duck-billed platypuses have an extra sense. They can detect electric currents. Test your electric sensitivity on a very dry day or on a winter day. Inflate a balloon. Rub the balloon against a wool sweater or the hair on your head. Hold a piece of tissue close to it. Can you see the tissue move toward it? Static electricity is causing the tissue to move toward the balloon. Rub the balloon against your hair again. Close your eyes and move it close to your bare arm or leg. How close does it have to get before you feel it? Why might it be useful to be able to sense electricity in the wild?

Your most important adaptation is your brain. The human brain helps us invent and use tools. Tools are things you can pick up or make when you need them and put down when you are done.

At first, humans used sticks, shells, and stones to help dig, break, and kill what they could. Humans learned to create much better tools, including hoes, axes, spear points, and wheels. These tools made life easier for humans. Now, we have many tools to help us every day. Can you think of some tools you use?

TRICKED YOU!

Some wild animals have developed their own tricks and tools to survive. For example, the margay is a wild cat that lives in Brazil and Central America. A margay will make sounds like a pied tamarin, which is a kind of small monkey. When the monkey comes out to investigate, the margay pounces on its dinner.

Many spiders trap their prey using sticky webs. Otters use rocks to open clam shells. Octopi hold on to coconut shells and use them as armor. Bottlenose dolphins use marine sponges to clean an area of the ocean floor when looking for food. Chimpanzees and crows will use special sticks to get insects that are hiding.

It doesn't matter if you are a predator or a prey animal. You are going to do what it takes to stay alive!

 CONSIDER AND DISCUSS

It's time to consider and discuss: What tools set humans apart from other predators?

PS Humpback whales can work together to make bubble nets that trap schools of herring. **You can see it in action in this video.** Do you think bubble nets work best when the whales are alone or in a group?

KEYWORD PROMPTS

National Geographic humpback whale bubble net

PROJECT!

POWER BOOST

SUPPLIES

* raw potato
* 2 to 3 drinking straws with stiff sides

Many animals use speed as a tool for catching or escaping. Long legs or wings or fins and strong muscles are needed for that. Speed can also give an animal a power boost when they need it. If you gently put your teeth down on a piece of hard candy, it takes a lot of work to break it. But if you open your mouth and then chomp down hard, the candy breaks apart easily.

1 Hold the potato in one hand and a straw in the other.

2 Put one finger over the end of the straw farthest away from the potato. This traps the air and makes the straw stiffer.

3 Put the straw on the side of the potato and try to push it through. What happens?

4 Keeping your finger over the far end of the straw, move the straw away from the potato, then quickly punch it toward the potato as fast and as hard as you can. It may take a bit of practice, but you should be able to punch the straw through the potato.

THINK ABOUT IT: The cheetah is the fastest land animal on the planet. When a cheetah attacks a gazelle, sometimes it can break its neck with one bite. Sharp teeth and strong jaws help, but the cheetah's speed gives it the power boost it needs.

PROJECT!

SPIDER WEBS

SUPPLIES

* paper plate
* scissors
* sticky tape (clear tape or masking tape) or Velcro
* hole punch
* string
* craft pom-pom balls of different sizes

Most spiders are known for their beautiful webs. These webs are made from sticky strands that hold onto anything that touches them. A waiting spider is alerted when the web starts to wiggle from a stuck animal trying to escape. The spider then rushes out, wraps its prey in more silk, and bites it. While biting, the spider squirts in a chemical that turns the insides of the prey to a liquid. A little while later, the spider can suck up its dinner. Yum!

1 Fold the paper plate in half. Cut a half circle in the center of the plate on the fold and open it up. You should have a circle cut out.

2 Spider web strands are sticky on both sides. Stick one edge of a piece of tape across the plate. Put another strand on the back side.

3 Make a pattern using at least five strands, but don't fill the entire area. Make sure there are some spaces big enough for your pom-pom prey animals to get through.

4 Punch four holes about the same distance apart around the edge of the plate.

┌ **Did You Know?** ─ ─ ─ ─ ─ ┐

Hummingbirds use spider webs to hold their nests together! Sometimes, they eat the spider that made the web first.

WORDS ⮕ KNOW

chemical: a substance that has certain features that can react with other substances.

PROJECT!

5 Cut four pieces of string, each about 18 inches long. (You can make them longer or shorter if you need to). These strings will hold the web in place. Tie one end of each string in a small hole near the edge of the paper plate. Tie the other ends to a branch, twig, or the side of chair.

6 Stand about 2 feet away from the web. Toss one pom-pom at a time toward the web. Does the pom-pom prey get caught or fly free? Which is more likely to make it through the web, smaller or larger pom-poms?

7 Research the different types of spider webs at this webpage. Try to recreate one of these webs on a paper plate and toss pom-poms through it. Which webs work the best to catch prey?

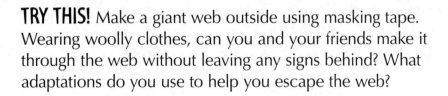

KEYWORD PROMPTS

National Geographic spider web patterns 🔍

TRY THIS! Make a giant web outside using masking tape. Wearing woolly clothes, can you and your friends make it through the web without leaving any signs behind? What adaptations do you use to help you escape the web?

CALLING ALL CRITTERS

SUPPLIES

* 2 quarters
* small cup
* drinking straw
* strip of paper

Hunters, photographers, and naturalists try to get deer, turkey, geese, owls, and other animals to come closer. They use boxes, horns, antlers, squawkers, and noises they make with their mouths. You can make easy callers that really work! Get your camera ready, and see what you can call.

1 This works best if you see a squirrel or two close by. Crouch or sit down. Put one quarter in each hand, and quickly strike the edges together several times. This will mimic their chatter.

2 Black-capped chickadees are common, curious birds. One of their calls is a high note followed by a lower note, sounding like it is saying, "fee-bee." If you hear a chickadee, stand still. Start making a kissing noise or saying, "pssssh, pssssh, psssh." The chickadee might come closer to see who is making that noise.

3 Wild turkeys are becoming more common around the United States. One has even been seen in Central Park in New York City! Try to find an area where you know turkeys are living. Look for parks or farm fields that have open areas with forest on the edge. Put the drinking straw in the cup. Hold it against the side wall and lift the straw so it is just above the bottom of the cup. Barely put the other end of the straw inside the corner of your lips. Suck in short bursts of air. It should tickle your lips, and sound like a turkey cluck.

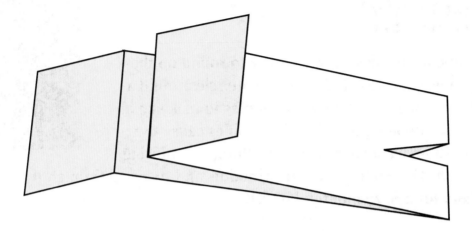

4 To make an alarm squawker, cut a strip of paper about 6 inches long and 2 inches wide. Fold the slip in half. Cut a small notch in the middle of the center fold. Bend the tips up and place one tip near each corner of your mouth. Blow hard toward the center notch. If you see the paper moving, but not making a sound, move the tips closer together. This alarm call will alert dogs, jays, and other animals.

THINK ABOUT IT: If you aren't successful in attracting any animals the first time, try again. Think about the time of day and season of the year. Remember, animals are not always active when you are!

PS Listen here to a black-capped chickadee!

KEYWORD PROMPTS

black-capped chickadee all about birds 🔍

PROJECT!

BUBBLE NET

Humpback whales work together to round up the fish they want to eat. They make a circle around a school of herring, then blow bubbles to make an air cage surrounding the fish. The bubbles cause the water to move up and down in columns, confusing the fish. The whales open their mouths and swim up through the school for a fizzy mouthful of fish.

Caution: Do not drink the detergent mixture.

1 Fill the bowl about half full with water and stir in one squirt of dish detergent. Gently stir the mixture using your straw. You can also substitute milk for the water and detergent mixture.

2 Place the floating prey in the bowl.

3 Place one end of the straw in the bowl and gently blow bubbles. How long does it take to get the prey animal surrounded?

4 Add more prey. Can you catch them all in the same bubble net or do some escape?

TRY THIS! Humpback whales work in groups of about 12. With a group of friends, fill a plastic swimming pool with water. Add ¼ cup of detergent and stir to mix. Scatter floating prey around the top. How well does your group work to bubble net dinner?

CHAPTER 3

EAT IT UP!

Both predators and prey need to get their food
into their bodies after finding or catching it.
How do you get food into your body?

Humans, monkeys, lemurs, raccoons, and pandas all can use
their hands to get food inside their bodies. Other animals use
lips, tongues, teeth, or beaks. If you look at the insides and
outsides of animal mouths,
what clues would you get
about what each animal eats?

? **INVESTIGATE!**

How would you get
food in your mouth if
you didn't have hands?

LIPS AND TONGUES

On the outside of your mouth are lips. You can see lips on most mammals and some fish. Birds and turtles have hard beaks instead of lips. Amphibians, reptiles, insects, crabs, worms, and many others don't have lips or beaks! But animals that do have lips put them to good use.

Your lips are soft and sensitive. You use your lips to smile, talk, whistle, blow bubbles, touch things, and to eat and drink. Monkeys and apes use their lips in many of the same ways.

Giraffes have super tough lips so they don't get hurt when they pull thorny branches into their mouths. Triggerfish and catfish have lips with taste buds on them. These help them find their prey. They eat the crabs and worms buried under the muck.

Snakes and some lizards have small holes to let their tongues slide through without opening their mouths. They use those flicking tongues to help them find their prey.

lure: an object, smell, or sound that attracts animals.

nutrients: the substances found in food that a plant or animal needs to live and grow.

WORDS TO KNOW

Tongues can be valuable tools for both predators and prey. Tongues can be long or short, sticky or dry, pointed or tube-like. They are used to smell, wrap, stick, pull, scrape, bite, and even glow!

HOW DO YOU SPELL MOUSETRAP WITH JUST THREE LETTERS?

C – A – T

Snakes and lizards use their tongues to help them smell. Giraffe tongues are so strong that they can pull leaves off trees! Cows can wrap their tongues around clumps of grass and tear them from the ground.

Hummingbirds use their tongues like tubes to pump up the nectar. Woodpeckers stick their stiff tongues into trees to get insects. Anteaters, pangolins, chameleons, and many frogs have long, sticky tongues that they use to catch the insects they eat. Penguins have spiny tongues to help them hold onto the fish they catch. Lions use their rough tongues to scrape meat off the bones of the animals they catch.

Some reptiles use their tongues as lures. When the tuatara fung-tongue opens its mouth, insects see its glow-in-the-dark tongue and fly right inside! Dinnertime!

Did You Know?

Some animals get their food inside without using a mouth! Zombie worms absorb nutrients from bones in the ocean. Pacific hagfish go inside rotting animals and the nutrients from the dead animal get into the hagfish through its skin!

WORDS TO KNOW

organ: a part of the body with a specific job. Organs include your heart, lungs, and skin.

SMELL WITH YOUR TONGUE

Snakes and monitor lizards have two holes in the roofs of their mouths, similar to your nose. These are part of Jacobsen's **organ**. They stick each tip of their forked tongues in one hole. This organ senses the chemicals on their tongues as smells. These tongues are so sensitive that snakes can tell if a smell is stronger coming from the right or left side of their heads! You can see a video of snakes using Jacobsen's organs here.

KEYWORD PROMPTS

snake secret weapon 🔍

← — — — — — —

BEAKS AND TEETH

Lips and tongues are great tools, but they might not work well on big or hard things. Time to call in beaks and teeth!

Owls, hawks, eagles, and falcons have thick, curved beaks that can rip their prey into pieces for swallowing. Herons and egrets have long, stabbing beaks that can snatch up fish, frogs, and snakes. These predators then fling the food into the air, open their mouths, and swallow it all, head first.

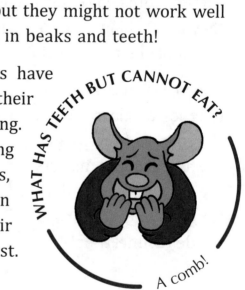

WHAT HAS TEETH BUT CANNOT EAT?

A comb!

incisor: a front, chisel-shaped tooth in mammals, used for cutting.

WORDS TO KNOW

Robins have beaks that can pluck worms from the ground. Woodpeckers have sharp, poking beaks to drill into trees. Many ducks and geese have beaks that look like teeth. The ridged edges help these birds strain their food out of the water.

In land mammals, the teeth in the front are called incisors. Humans have eight incisors, four on the top and four on the bottom. Incisors have straight edges on the tips and are shaped like wedges. These teeth are used to bite or snip things.

Did You Know?

In rodents, including beavers, squirrels, mice, and guinea pigs, the four incisors keep growing while the animal is alive.

Many grass-eating animals, including deer and bison, have incisors only on their bottom jaws. They eat by pulling a clump of grass into their mouths with their tongues. Then they snip off the clump by pushing the bottom incisors against the bone in their upper jaws. In elephants, the top incisors grow extra-long and become tusks.

Humans also have four canine teeth, one on each side, top and bottom. These teeth are longer and stronger than the other teeth, and can be pointy. They are used for ripping and tearing tough things, such as steak.

Since herbivores eat only plants, many of them don't have any canines. There are gaps in their jaws where these teeth would be.

The canine teeth in omnivores are often a bit longer than the other teeth. Most mammal predators have extra big canines. This helps identify them as carnivores, or meat eaters.

Next are your big, almost square, chewing, mashing teeth. These are called premolars and molars. An animal's molars can offer a big hint about what that animal eats. Most herbivore prey animals have flat molars on the top and bottom that meet together like Lego blocks. These are used to chew food into smaller bits to make it easier to digest.

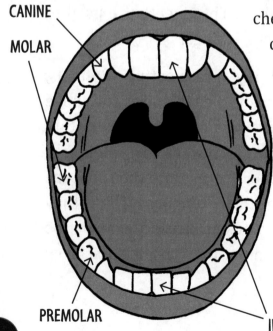

CANINE

MOLAR

PREMOLAR

INCISOR

TEETH IN THE OCEAN

Whales, dolphins, and porpoises do not have the same type of teeth as land predators. Instead of having three or four different kinds of teeth working together, all the teeth are the same.

Clam-eating zebra sharks have flat teeth, while fish-eating shortfin mako sharks have thin, pointy teeth. Great white sharks and others that eat sea lions, dolphins, and even small whales have triangular teeth that help them tear their prey apart.

Sharks and snakes have teeth that are easily pulled out. That is okay, because they grow new teeth whenever they need to. Some sharks get new teeth every two weeks!

The biggest predator in the world doesn't have any teeth at all! The great blue whale has baleen. These are long, flexible, fingernail-like combs that trap tiny animals inside a whale's mouth when it pushes out a gulp of ocean water.

> **baleen:** the tough, flexible material hanging down in some whales' mouths to help trap their food.
>
> ### WORDS TO KNOW

? CONSIDER AND DISCUSS

It's time to consider and discuss: How would you get food in your mouth if you didn't have hands?

PROJECT!

LIP SERVICE

Most animals' lips are attached to their jaws. Humans have lips that are loose. Attached lips are sturdier, but loose lips can move more. Put your lips to the test and see how valuable they are to you!

SUPPLIES

- science journal and pencil
- paper clip
- ruler
- cotton ball
- drinking glass
- warm water
- ice cube
- drinking straws of different sizes

Caution: Be very careful with the sharp ends of the paper clip.

1 Uncurl the paper clip and make it into a U shape.

2 Close your eyes and gently press both tips of the clip to your lower lip. Can you feel one or two points? Measure and record the distance between the tips and whether you felt one or two points. You can use a table like the one shown below to organize your data.

	Distance	Felt one point	Felt two points
Lower Lip			
Lower Lip			
Lower Lip			
Upper Lip			
Upper Lip			
Upper Lip			

3 Make the distance between the tips larger or smaller and repeat the test. Record your results and repeat until you know the distance at which it feels like just one point.

4 Repeat this test on your upper lip. Are your results the same?

5 Dip a cotton ball in a glass of warm water and press this on your lips. Repeat the test. Do your results change?

6 Rub an ice cube on your lips. Repeat the test. Do your results change?

7 Put one end of a drinking straw in a glass of water. Put the other end in your mouth. Try to take a drink without closing your lips around the straw. How did you do? Try a different size.

Did You Know?

Many land predators have pointy molars called carnassials. These teeth interlock. Some predators use these teeth to hold onto their prey so it can't escape.

THINK ABOUT IT: Why do you think lips need to be sensitive in the wild? How does this adaptation help with survival?

WORDS TO KNOW

carnassial: a square-shaped, sharp-pointed tooth in the middle and back of carnivorous mammal jaws.

TONGUE TWISTER

Frogs are known for the super-fast, sticky tongues they use to catch flies, other insects, and even small birds and mammals. Try catching dinner using a tongue substitute!

1 Use your hands to unroll the party blower. Turn it upside down and weigh the ends down with a book.

2 Attach a hook piece from one of the sticky-back Velcro dots to the tip of the blower. Let the blower curl back up. This is your frog tongue.

3 Cut the felt into pieces of different sizes. Use the permanent marker to draw an animal that a frog might eat on each one.

4 Place the prey pieces on a table, floor, or have them cling to a curtain or lampshade. Try to catch each prey piece with your frog tongue. Is there a limit to the size of prey it can pick up?

TRY THIS! Design a stronger frog tongue. How about a longer frog tongue? What happens if you add more Velcro dots to your frog tongue? Can you catch more prey?

PUMP IT UP!

What do flamingos and great blue whales have in common? They are both filter feeders. They get a mouth full of water and animals. Then, they push their tongues and cheeks to move the water out through their filters, leaving dinner behind in their mouths.

1 Fill one bowl half full with water. Add glitter.

2 Take the cap off the bottle. Squeeze in the sides. Holding the bottle with the sides squeezed in, put the mouth of the bottle in the water. Release your grip on the sides.

3 Tilt the bottle upright as you lift it from the bowl so you don't spill much.

4 Use the rubber band to hold the piece of gauze in place over the bottle mouth.

5 Put the bottle over the empty bowl. Squeeze the sides to push the water out. Remove the gauze and look at your dinner!

TRY THIS! Experiment with different bottle coverings, such as a comb, different fabrics, a window screen, and a bottle cap with holes punched in it. What else can you use as a filter? What works best? Make a chart and record the results in your journal.

PROJECT!

MOUTH MODEL

SUPPLIES

* ✳ science journal and pencil
* ✳ scissors
* ✳ egg carton
* ✳ cardboard
* ✳ clay
* ✳ craft sticks
* ✳ candy corn
* ✳ other items you find

Many animals use their teeth to tear their food apart. Beavers, mice, and squirrels have big, sharp front incisors that can cut pieces out of hard shells or trees. The incisors on predators are usually much smaller and are used to hold or snip small bites. The canines on herbivores are missing, while canines on carnivores can be super long and thick. The molars and premolars are shaped to either chew food into mushy bits or just get it down the hatch.

1 Design a model of a mouth. What kind of animal do you want to represent? A predator? An herbivore? An omnivore? Research the animal you want to model, then get creative! Write notes and draw pictures in your science journal of the mouth model you want to make.

2 An egg carton makes a terrific base. You can cut off sections and glue them on cardboard or use just the top or just the bottom. The egg cups make great carnassials. If you are making the mouth of a prey animal with flat molars, use paper or clay to fill in between them.

3 One way to make incisors is to cut craft sticks into shorter pieces. Push them through the carton and glue in place.

Did You Know?

Humans only grow one set of molars in their lives. Elephants can grow new molars six times during their lifetimes!

44

MAKE AN APPLE MOLD

Ask an adult to slice an apple for you. Put the slice in your mouth so the curved outside edge (with the apple peel) is just outside your lips. Bite down, but don't bite through! Take the apple out of your mouth and look at the pattern of your teeth. Sketch your bite marks in your journal. Compare it with others. Measure it. Are any of your teeth missing? Which teeth do you use to take a bite out of a whole apple? Do you have any pointy teeth? Which teeth chew gum?

4 If your model needs canine teeth, use dagger-shaped items such as candy corn or the corner of a broken cracker. Glue these in place between the incisors and back teeth.

5 Be sure to take a picture of your mouth model! Can your friends guess what kind of animal has this mouth?

THINK ABOUT IT: Fish and snakes don't have hands or feet. Their teeth are curved to help them hold onto their food. What could you use to model this type of teeth?

CHAPTER 4

STAYING SAFE

When a predator chases an animal, the prey doesn't just roll over and die. It fights back! At the same time, predators don't want to get hurt while fighting another animal. Many predators are also prey. They can be eaten by even bigger predators!

Both predators and prey work to stay safe. Sometimes, they stay safe by choosing when to be active, day or night. They also carefully choose where to make their homes. Many prey animals have developed extra defenses. The trouble is, there always seems to be a predator with a way around those defenses.

? INVESTIGATE!

What are some strategies you use to stay safe at home and at school?

defense: protection from attack.

musk: a strong-smelling odor from the musk deer or another animal.

WORDS ᴛᴏ KNOW

PEE-YEW!

Some animals make a stink about staying safe. Millipedes eat dead leaves, fungi, and sometimes rotting animals. They are surrounded by smelly stuff. However, that doesn't stop predators from eating them. As protection, some millipedes release a smell so harmful that it can kill a mouse!

Skunks are another animal known for creating a stink. This keeps away most predators, but not great horned owls. Owls do not have a very good sense of smell. An owl doesn't care if its prey stinks, as long as it tastes good.

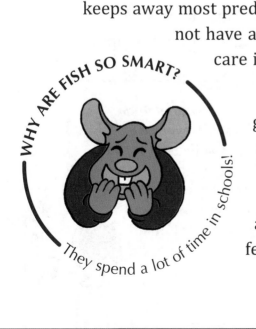

WHY ARE FISH SO SMART?

They spend a lot of time in schools!

Garter snakes also release nasty smelling goo if they are attacked. After eating, a wolverine will spray its leftover prey with a strong musk to keep other animals from eating it. The terrible smell released by anteaters can be noticed more than 50 feet away!

diurnal: active during the day.

WORDS TO KNOW

BODIES TO THE RESCUE

Instead of smells, some animals use the shape of their bodies to stay safe. Flounder fish are flat and swim along the bottom of the ocean. This makes them harder to see and grab. Pufferfish might look good to eat until they inhale a lot of water and air. Then they look like a big, poky balloon!

The porcupine is a land mammal with spiky quills. When a predator threatens, it will raise its quills. If the predator brushes against the quills, the quills can get stuck in its skin. Ouch!

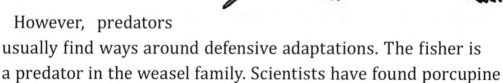

However, predators usually find ways around defensive adaptations. The fisher is a predator in the weasel family. Scientists have found porcupine quills in fisher poop. Porcupines don't have quills on the nose or the belly, so fishers either bite the nose and flip it over or attack its belly while it is in a tree.

> **Did You Know?**
> If there are few predators around, rabbits will be diurnal, or active during the day. If they do not feel safe during the day because of hunting hawks or coyotes, they become nocturnal.

SAFETY IN NUMBERS

Another way predator and prey animals try to survive is by working in groups. Wolves hunt together in family packs. These packs can take down animals bigger than they are, such as bison or elk. Sometimes, there is enough meat on these kills to feed all the animals in the pack for several days.

On the prey side, some animals are usually alone. These include woodchucks, koalas, and red squirrels. Being alone makes it easier to hide or escape the attention of predators.

Others, including bison, snow geese, and some fish, gather in big groups. These groups don't try to hide. Instead, big groups make it harder for predators to find the young, old, injured, and sick animals that are easier to kill.

Instead of hanging out in large groups, some predator and prey animals stick together as family units. Baby kangaroos spend most of their time in their mothers' pouches until they are about six months old. Alligators carry their young around in their mouths or on their heads.

WORDS TO KNOW

toxin: a poison that can cause sickness or death.

venom: a poison made by some animals that is injected into other animals to cause pain or death.

WOLVES IN YELLOWSTONE NATIONAL PARK

Some prey will change their behavior when predators are around. For years, there were no wolves in Yellowstone National Park. The elk and deer could go wherever they wanted. When wolves were reintroduced, the elk and deer didn't know how to act. They quickly learned they were safer if they stayed out of valleys. This meant the grasses and other plants in the valleys had a chance to grow, because the deer weren't nibbling it down. You can see a video about this at this website.

KEYWORD PROMPTS

Yellowstone wolf river 🔍

POISON CONTROL

Toxins are an effective adaptation used by both predator and prey. Toxins are chemicals that can hurt or kill an animal. Predators, such as some snakes, short-tailed shrews, and tarantula hawk wasps, inject venom into an animal. The venom slows the animal down so it is easy to catch it, paralyze it, and kill it.

Some animals use poisons for protection. Prey animals use poison to make the predators that eat them get sick or even die.

immune: able to resist a disease or a toxin.

WORDS ⊕ KNOW

Poison dart frogs have poison on their skin and puffer fish have poison in their spines. Slow loris parents make a poison that they can lick off their bodies and onto their babies. This makes their babies poisonous to eat!

The sea wasp is one of the most venomous box jellyfish in the ocean. It uses the venom on the long strands under its body to catch small fish and shrimp. Flower urchins look like a pretty clump of flowers in a coral reef, but don't try to pick one up! It has small spines that poke poison into you that causes a lot of pain!

r ¬ **Did You Know?** – – ¬

The fire-bellied snake is the only animal immune to the golden dart frog's poison.

Animals have developed ways around venoms and poisons. Mongoose, honey badgers, secretary birds, hedgehogs, and opossums are at least somewhat immune to snake venom. Their bodies have certain chemicals that make the venom not work. If a venomous snake attacks them, they might turn around and eat the snake!

? **CONSIDER AND DISCUSS**

It's time to consider and discuss: What are some strategies you use to stay safe at home and at school?

51

PROJECT!

HERD OF SCHOOL?

There are animals that find safety in numbers. Instead of hiding, these animals form large groups. If a predator comes near, the group will surround the young, old, injured, and sick animals that the predator wants to chase. Does being in a group make it harder for a predator to find and catch a single prey?

1 In your journal, write down the question, "How many marbles makes a group big enough to hide one prey marble for one minute?" Record your hypothesis and any research you do.

2 Make a table for your results like the one below.

Number of marbles	Time it took to catch the prey	Observations

3 Find the smallest marble or one that has a chip or a crack. This will be your prey.

4 Sit in the chair. Put your prey marble in the box. Place the box on the tray. Place the tray on your knees and gently wiggle your knees. Start your timer and time how long it takes to catch your prey. Record that number in your journal.

5 Repeat the test using your prey marble plus five other marbles of different sizes and colors. Record how long it takes to catch your prey. Write down your observations. Was it easier or harder to catch your prey? Why?

6 Repeat the test using 10 marbles plus your prey. Record your results and observations.

7 Keep repeating the test, adding 10 marbles each round until you have used all your marbles. If you were a prey animal, would you rather travel in a group or by yourself?

TRY THIS! To simulate a herd of bison, repeat the activity putting the marbles directly on the tray and not in the box. Record your hypothesis before you do the tests. Was your hypothesis correct?

Did You Know?

Groups of animals are given different names. Check out this list of crazy group names.

Name	Animals
Herd	Cows, bison, llamas, sheep
School	Fish
Pack	Wolves
Embarrassment	Pandas
Creep	Tortoises
Constellation	Starfish
Congress	Owls
Murder	Crows

PROJECT!

GET IN SHAPE!

Some animals use their body coverings and shape as protection. Design an animal that is difficult for a predator to swallow!

1 Do some research on the colors and body parts of real animals.

2 Color the inside of the bottle by pouring a small amount of paint inside. Put the cap on the bottle and swirl it around until paint covers the sides. Pour out the extra paint. Leave the cap off and let the paint inside the bottle dry.

3 Make legs, fins, wings, ears, and other body parts using pipe cleaners, paper, and glue.

4 Ask an adult to help you use the tip of the scissors to cut slits in the bottle where you would like to attach the body parts.

5 Finish decorating your animal using the permanent markers.

SUPPLIES

* plastic drink bottle with lid
* paint
* hole punch
* pipe cleaners
* paper
* scissors
* glue
* permanent markers
* masking tape or fabric headband

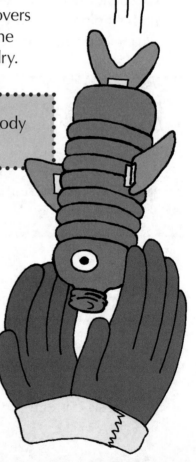

54

6 Hold your hands with the palms together. Ask a friend to wrap a band of masking tape around your hands near the base of your thumbs. You can also double up a large fabric headband. You now have a bird beak that can open only so far.

7 Imagine you just caught your bottle animal and you must swallow it head first to avoid getting jabbed. Toss it into the air and try to catch it with the head pointed down toward your hands.

TRY THIS! Design a way to make your animal get larger or to release a smell when grabbed. What materials would you use? What would your design be?

TINY PROTECTIVE GEAR

How would you like to wear a suit of armor? From the giant Indian rhinoceros to the tiny, roly poly bugs you can find living under logs around your home, many animals have hard plates covering their backs. These plates are small and narrow so the animals can move. They are also hard and stiff to provide a tough cover! Other animals with these hard plates include armadillos and pangolins. Scientists believe even some dinosaurs had hard, protective plates protecting their bodies!

NEUTRALIZE THAT

Venoms and poisons are chemicals that can hurt a body or change how it works. Some animals or plants make other chemicals that act against the venoms and poisons. Make and test this simple cabbage broth to see how this works!

Caution: An adult must help with the hot liquid.

1 In your science journal, create a chart to keep track of the color changes.

2 Tear the cabbage leaves into the smallest pieces possible. An adult can help if you want to use a grater or blender. Try to get about ¼ cup of tiny pieces.

3 Put the pieces in the microwave-safe bowl. Add just enough water to cover them.

4 Cook the cabbage until the water is starting to bubble. This takes less than 60 seconds on high.

5 Put on the oven mitt and remove the bowl from the microwave. Have an adult help. Let it cool for about 5 minutes.

SUPPLIES

* science journal and pencil
* fresh red cabbage leaves
* ¼ measuring cup
* microwave-safe bowl
* water
* microwave
* oven mitt
* strainer
* clear plastic cups, bowls, or bottles
* vinegar
* baking soda
* other chemicals to try, such as lemon juice, apple juice, soda, coffee, milk, dish soap, antacid
* grater or blender (optional)

PROJECT!

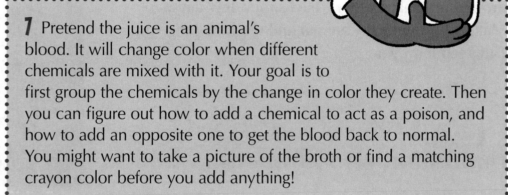

6 Pour the juice through a strainer and into another bowl or clear cup. Put the cooked cabbage leaves into your compost bin or garbage.

7 Pretend the juice is an animal's blood. It will change color when different chemicals are mixed with it. Your goal is to first group the chemicals by the change in color they create. Then you can figure out how to add a chemical to act as a poison, and how to add an opposite one to get the blood back to normal. You might want to take a picture of the broth or find a matching crayon color before you add anything!

THINK ABOUT IT: Imagine you are a predator of a baby slow loris. The mother has licked the baby with her chemical poison that would turn your juice blue. What could you put on the fur to get it back to normal?

ANTI-VENOM

When the venom is very strong, doctors might give a shot of anti-venom. Snake anti-venom is made by milking a snake. A person had to get a venomous snake to open its mouth and squirt its venom into a bottle. The venom is made weaker, then a small amount is shot into a horse, sheep, or goat. That animal's blood fights against the venom and makes anti-venom. When scientists take some of that blood, they can give the anti-venom to people.

PROJECT!

CLING ON

Little brown bats hang onto their mothers for a few days after they are born, even when the mother is flying around. Baby wolf spiders ride around on their mothers' backs for a few days. Make your own baby animal and see how long you can keep it on you.

1 Glue the googly eyes to the pom-pom and set aside to dry.

2 Cut the right number of legs from one or two pipe cleaners. You can bend each piece to make elbows and knees or hands and feet. Glue them to the pom-pom.

3 Find a way to carry your animal on you at all times. You can wear it or find a way to keep it safe in a pocket or bag.

4 If you want to wear your animal as a ring, wrap a long pipe cleaner around one finger. Twist the two ends together. Remove the ring and glue the pom-pom animal on the twisted ends to hide them.

PROJECT!

5 If you want to wear your animal as a pin, cut a piece of pipe cleaner to glue to the bottom of the pom-pom animal. Glue the back portion of the safety pin to the pipe cleaner.

6 After the glue has dried completely, put on the ring or pin. Be sure to protect your baby from getting hurt! And make sure it goes everywhere with you, even to bed!

TRY THIS! Use a camera or smartphone to take pictures of places you go with your baby animal. Write a story about its adventures—including any near misses with potential predators! Did a cat see it and want to play? Did it almost get knocked off while you were on the playground?

> **Did You Know?**
>
> **Baby orangutans never leave their mothers for the first four months of their lives, not even to eat, sleep, take a bath, and go to the bathroom!**

HANG ON!

Many cling-on animals are marsupials. These are animals that are born blind and hairless. They crawl into pouches on their mothers' bellies and stay there drinking milk until they are bigger. When the baby is big enough to come out, it often hangs onto mom for a few more weeks as it learns about the outside world. Marsupials include koalas, kangaroos, and opossums. You can see a young koala cling onto its mom and then go back in her pouch!

KEYWORD PROMPTS

Koala joey adorable-ness at Australia Zoo 🔍

CHAPTER 5

OTHER ANIMAL EATERS

Predators kill the animals they eat, but they are not the only animal eaters. There are some animals that find and eat creatures that are already dead. Called scavengers, these animals include opossums, hyenas, and vultures.

Have you ever been bitten by a mosquito? There are some animals that eat part of another animal without killing it. Vampire bats, mosquitoes, leeches, ticks, and some worms do this. These are called parasites.

 INVESTIGATE!

If mosquitoes disappeared, what effect could that have on other animals and the ecosystem?

There are even some plants that trap and eat animals. Venus fly traps, bladderworts, and pitcher plants are all called carnivorous plants. Just like other predators, these living things have special ways of finding, trapping, or getting to their food.

SCAVENGERS

Scavengers play a very important role in the natural world. Every day, animals die in many different ways. They might run into a window or get sick. Sometimes, they die because there is not enough food or water.

Floods and fires kill some animals, while cars and old age kill others. Some get killed by predators, but the predator might not eat the entire animal.

This is where those scavengers come in. They are the earth's cleanup crew!

scavenger: an animal that feeds on animals that are already dead.

parasite: a plant or animal that feeds on another plant or animal without directly killing it.

ecosystem: a community of plants and animals living in an area, relying on each other to survive.

carnivorous plant: a plant that traps and eats animals.

WORDS TO KNOW

Vultures, burying beetles, and yellow jackets are true scavengers—they don't hunt and kill at all. They just find and eat what is already dead. They are carnivores, but not predators.

Some scavengers follow predators around. They wait until the predator leaves its kill, then move in for the leftovers.

Some flies and beetles can smell an animal almost as soon as it has died. They might feed on the dead body. They might also lay eggs on the body so that their babies can feed on the dead meat.

> ### Did You Know?
>
> **Bears, coyotes, hyenas, and raccoons are both predators and scavengers. These animals will hunt, but they will also eat animals that are already dead.**

Some animals, such as vultures, usually find animals that have been dead for a few days. Vultures have a good sense of smell that helps them find their meals.

DO YOU SMELL SOMETHING?

Natural gas is used by people to heat their homes, power their stoves, and even run their vehicles. Some companies send the gas through long pipes over the land. This gas can cause an explosion if there is a lot of it around a flame. To keep people safer, natural gas companies add a chemical smell to the gas. The smell is similar to that of a dead animal. Not only does this let people smell the leaks, it also alerts vultures! If workers see vultures circling over an area of pipe, they go to see if there is a leak.

PARASITES

There are some animals that need to feed on other animals, but they only need certain parts, not the entire animal. Parasites catch and eat just part of an animal.

A female mosquito only needs a tiny drink of blood, not an entire animal. It doesn't intentionally kill its victim, it just gives the animal a little poke. Then it sticks in its tube, pumps in a little saliva to keep the blood flowing, sucks out some blood, and leaves. The victim might be a bit itchy, but it will likely stay alive and make more blood.

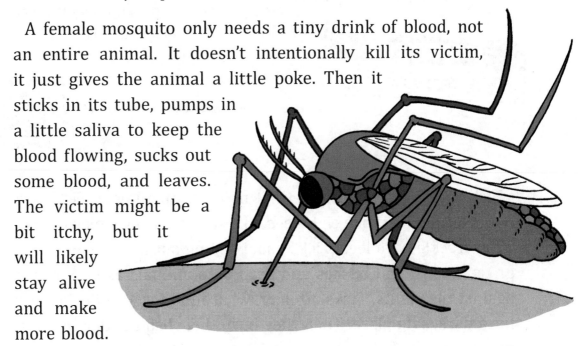

TWO VULTURES ARE IN A FIELD, EATING A DEAD CLOWN. ONE VULTURE SAYS TO THE OTHER . . . "Does this taste funny to you?"

Another blood-thirsty parasite is the vampire bat. Instead of sucking out its blood meal with a tube, a vampire bat bites the ankles or legs of a cow or other large mammal. It gets its food by licking the blood that oozes out. The animal it bit keeps on living and producing more blood—which means more food for more bats!

minerals: nutrients found in rocks and soil that keep plants and animals healthy and growing. Salt and nitrogen are two minerals.

WORDS TO KNOW

SAY "AHHHHHH . . ."

There are parasites that eat things other than blood. The tongue-eating louse, a tiny parasite that gets inside a fish's mouth, eats the tongue. Then it takes the place of the tongue! You can see pictures of this parasite at this website.

KEYWORD PROMPTS

tongue-eating fish parasite 🔍

Ticks are another parasite that many people know. Ticks are not insects. They have eight legs, like spiders. They look a bit like a flat freckle with legs. Ticks usually hang out in areas with tall grass, weeds, and bushes and grab onto animals as they brush against the plants. Ticks often crawl around for a while, looking for a dark, safe place. Then they bury their head under the skin to get a drink of blood. Some can keep drinking for several days! Most ticks can feed on many other animals, not just humans. They can spread disease, such as Lyme disease, that can affect both humans and animals.

PREDATOR PLANTS

Most plants make their own food. Plants use sunlight and minerals from the soil and water as ingredients. However, some places don't have enough minerals in the soil and water. Many plants die in these places.

Did You Know?

Lyme disease comes from a bacteria that is carried by deer ticks. Animals and people who get this disease can feel very tired and their arms and legs can feel sore. That's why it's important to check for ticks whenever you come in from playing outside!

Some plants have developed a different adaptation to get their minerals—by eating animals! These carnivorous plants include sundews, pitcher plants, and Venus fly traps.

Plants have to lure their prey to them. All kinds of plants make nectar to attract insects. In most plants, the insect takes a drink of the nectar, gets brushed with pollen, and then flies or crawls away. In carnivorous plants, the insect comes in to get a drink of nectar and gets trapped.

Sundews have sticky leaves that act like flypaper. Pitcher plants have tiny pools of slippery liquid. Venus fly traps have hinged leaves that snap shut when an insect trips a trigger hair.

Carnivorous plants have a special nectar that makes the animal turn into liquid. Then the plant absorbs that liquid and uses the minerals to help it make its food.

? CONSIDER AND DISCUSS

It's time to consider and discuss: If mosquitoes disappeared, what effect could that have on other animals and the ecosystem?

MAKE A MODEL PITCHER PLANT

There is an old saying, "You can catch more flies with honey than with vinegar." Here is a chance to see if that is true. Make this model of a pitcher plant. Which nectar do you think will attract the most insects, vinegar or honey?

SUPPLIES

* science journal and pencil
* clean plastic drink bottle, any size
* permanent marker
* scissors
* tablespoon
* vinegar
* honey

Caution: Have an adult help you cut the bottle.

1 On the front of one of the large, double-spread sheets in your journal, write "Pitcher Plant Test." Follow the scientific method and record your hypothesis.

2 Use the permanent marker to draw a line around the bottle just below where the mouth gets wide.

3 Holding the bottle on the top of a table or desk, use the tip of the scissors to poke a hole through the bottle on the line. Cut all the way around the bottle on the line.

4 Pour about 2 tablespoons of vinegar into the bottle. Turn the top of the bottle upside down and nest it in the bottle bottom.

5 Put your pitcher plant model outside in an area that is not windy. Just like a real pitcher plant, once an insect flies or crawls in, it will have a hard time getting out, unless you take the top off.

PROJECT!

6 While you are waiting to see if any insects visit, open your journal to your Pitcher Plant Test. On the left-hand page, draw a chart to record your vinegar findings. On the right-hand page, draw a chart to record your honey findings. Be sure to label each page and to note the time you set out the trap.

7 After a full 24 hours (there are insects out day and night!), check the trap. After counting and identifying the insects in the trap, remove the funnel part to release them.

8 Take the trap inside and clean it with soap and water. After drying it, add about 2 tablespoons of honey to the trap and take it to the same place.

9 Leave the trap in place for a full 24 hours. Then check and record the results.

10 Compare your results. Do you think they would change if you left the trap out for a longer period of time?

THINK ABOUT IT: What kind of insects visited your pitcher plant? Check out this online guide to help you identify some possible visitors to your pitcher plant. Were different types of insects attracted to the vinegar and the honey?

KEYWORD PROMPTS

bug facts 🔍

PROJECT!

SCAVENGER HUNT

SUPPLIES

✳ science journal and pencil

There are often dead flies in window frames, flat squirrels in the street, and beat-up butterflies on the front grills of cars. Scientists record information about dead animals to keep track of which animals are around, how they might be moving from one place to another, and even to check on their health. Scientists can see if a dead animal had a disease, parasites, and many other things. By doing a dead animal survey in your area, you become an honorary member of the Super Scavenger Club!

Caution: Do not touch dead animals.

1 Open your journal to an empty page. Title it "Dead Animal Scavenger Hunt." Copy this chart on the page.

Type of animal	Predator or prey?	Location	Condition (run over, mummy . . .)	Cause of death (if known)

PROJECT!

2 Decide how big an area you want to survey and for how long.

3 Walk around your survey area, looking for bodies or signs of dead animals. Those signs might include a ball of silk in a spider web, a dragonfly wing on the ground, or even a chewed bone.

4 When you find a dead animal, don't pick it up. It might have something harmful on it. Simply record your findings on your chart. At times, you might not be able to fill in every section of the table. Sometimes, you might only find a few scraps of fur or a bone. Do the best you can.

5 Repeat this test at different times of the year. Do you notice any changes?

TRY THIS! With an adult's permission, you can become a citizen scientist! Join a roadkill survey crew to help road planners reduce the number of animals killed by cars.

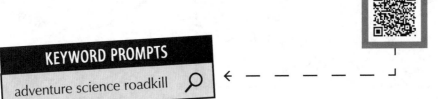

KEYWORD PROMPTS

adventure science roadkill 🔍

PROJECT!

SUCK IT UP!

Mosquitoes, leeches, ticks, and vampire bats are a few of the parasites that feed on the blood of other animals. When you get a scrape or cut your skin, your body makes clots to stop blood from gushing out. Clots are like thick plugs that jam up the hole. Blood-loving parasites have a special chemical in their saliva that slows down the making of blood clots. This lets the parasite drink easier for a longer time. With the help of an adult, you can see how this works with an edible activity.

1 Use the marker or tape to label one cup "fresh" and the other cup "saliva injected."

2 Put two to three pieces of fresh or frozen fruit in the cup marked saliva injected. Use a spoon to smash them to get the juice out. Pick out the fruit, leaving the juice behind. The fruit juice will act as the clot stopper.

WHAT DO YOU CALL A FLY WITHOUT WINGS?

A walk!

3 Ask an adult to help you. Follow the directions on the gelatin package to make the gelatin in the bowl. This will be your fake blood.

4 When the gelatin is mixed, pour a small amount into each cup. Put both cups in a refrigerator for at least one hour.

5 Remove the cups from the refrigerator. Time how long it takes to suck up all the blood from each cup using the straw. Record your observations in your journal.

THINK ABOUT IT: As you probably know from experience, you don't keep bleeding from a mosquito bite unless you scratch it! The human body is pretty big compared to the parasites it attracts. After a while, the mosquito's saliva is either flushed out of the body or overwhelmed by unaffected blood, and a clot forms. Design a way to flush the pineapple juice out of the gelatin. How can you get it out of your cup so the gelatin becomes harder to suck?

Did You Know?

Mosquitoes don't actually bite you. They stab you, spit in a bit of saliva, and suck your blood.

CHAPTER 6

LIVING TOGETHER

• •

For hundreds of years, people have been studying animal populations all around the world. Some of the studies have been done by landowners who keep track of the wildlife in their area. Some studies have been done by famous scientists, including Charles Darwin and Aldo Leopold. Some studies have been done by people who are simply curious! Many scientists, including Bill Ripple and Lynne Gilbert-Norton, are still studying predators and prey because it's such an important topic.

• •

? INVESTIGATE!

How do humans change the balance between predators and prey?

endangered: a plant or animal with a very low population that is at risk of disappearing entirely.

WORDS TO KNOW

RELATIONSHIP PATTERNS

There have been many results from these studies. One interesting idea is that there are patterns in the relationships between the number of predators and the number of prey. All of the different ecosystems around the world depend on having a balance of predator and prey animals.

If there are too many predators, they eat too many prey animals. Then they don't have enough food and they starve. If there are too many prey animals, they eat too many of the plants. When there aren't enough plants around to feed everyone, the prey animals starve. If the plants disappear, the whole habitat can be changed.

In some cases, people have introduced animals to places where they don't naturally live. European settlers took rabbits to Australia to eat and to hunt. The rabbits didn't have any natural predators and started taking over the habitat.

When people realized they couldn't control the rabbit population, they released cats. The cats hunted the rabbits, but the cats also hunted many other animals native to Australia. These animals didn't have any defenses against cats. Now some of these native animals are endangered.

ecologist: a scientist
who studies plants and
animals and their habitat.

WORDS TO KNOW

KEEPING THE BALANCE

Many wildlife ecologists are trying to think of new ways to make sure habitats stay healthy and in balance. For example, many cities have lots of rats and pigeons. These animals are not afraid of humans. They can also carry diseases that can hurt humans or pets.

Instead of using traps and poisons to solve these problems, some cities are trying to attract predators. Owl houses are being placed in city parks. Nests for peregrine falcons are put on tall city buildings in New York City, Chicago, Atlanta, San Francisco, and more than 20 other cities. These predators help with the problem of city pests.

┌ Did You Know? – – – – – – – – – – – –

House cats that roam outdoors are one of the biggest predator problems in cities in the United States and Great Britain. These cats kill millions of songbirds and small mammals each year. Unlike wild predators, these cats also have food at home, so they are not likely to starve.

THE KAIBAB PLATEAU

In 1906, people decided they wanted to protect the deer in the Kaibab Plateau in northern Arizona. They outlawed hunting the deer, and hunted the cougars, wolves, coyote, and bobcats that preyed on the deer instead. The number of deer more than doubled. By 1920, many deer were dying because they could not find enough food to eat. Even after many deer died, the habitat did not recover.

Wolves were released in Yellowstone National Park in 1995. They had been hunted out of the park more than 70 years earlier. They were brought back, in part, to prey on the elk herds, which were too big.

The wolves did hunt elk and other animals in Yellowstone. But farmers and ranchers near Yellowstone worry that the wolves will eat their sheep and cows, too.

Scientists are studying ways to keep predators from hunting these animals. They are trying noise boxes and waving flags. Some farmers are adding llamas or donkeys to their herds of sheep to act as protectors.

WHAT IS THE BEST WAY TO GET RID OF A 100-POUND WORM IN YOUR GARDEN?

Get a 1,000-pound robin!

? CONSIDER AND DISCUSS

It's time to consider and discuss:
How do humans change the balance between predators and prey?

GO FISH!

Scientists have noticed that humans can change the balance of predators and prey in an area more than any other animal. To keep our ecosystems healthy, it is important for people to plan how many animals they hunt. Play this new version of Go Fish and see how well you do as a wildlife manager!

Rules:

- The pond can sustain 16 fish.

- If you get more than 16 fish for more than two rounds in a row, the fish food will run out and all the fish will die.

- You need at least two fish to be alive at the end of every round to mate and have more fish.

- You need to catch three fish each round to stay alive.

1 Make a chart like the one on the next page in your journal.

2 Count 16 goldfish crackers and place them in the bowl. Write "16" in the first box in your chart.

3 Set your timer for 15 seconds. Use a spoon or chopsticks to try to catch fish one at a time. Put the fish you catch in the cup.

4 When time is up, count how many fish you caught and record this number in your chart.

PROJECT!

Round	# of fish in pond	# of fish you catch	Do you live? 3+ fish	# of fish remaining	# fish you add 2x fish remaining
1	16	4	yes	12	24
2	36				
3					
4					

5 You need three fish to stay alive. If you caught at least three fish, continue. If not, start again.

Did You Know?

Snowy owls live in Canada, where their main food is lemmings. When there are too many owls and not enough lemmings, the owls fly south to find other food.

6 Count the number of remaining fish in the bowl. If there are fewer than two fish, the game is over. If there are two or more fish, for every fish still in the bowl, add two more. The fish had babies!

7 Count the number of fish in the bowl after adding more. Record that number in the first box on the second line.

8 Set the timer for another 15 seconds and play another round. How many rounds can you play before you starve or the pond is too full?

BALANCING ACT

The earth needs both predators and prey. The location and number of each may change each year, but through time, they balance out. How well can you balance them?

1 Place the coat hanger over the paper and trace around the outside of the center triangle.

2 Use the markers to draw a habitat in the triangle—ocean, field, forest, or city. Cut around the outside edge of the triangle.

3 Use the hole punch to make a hole about 2 inches away from each bottom corner and 1 inch above the bottom edge.

4 Tape the paper to the center triangle in the hanger. Do not cover up the holes.

5 Poke a pipe cleaner through each hole. Bend each top edge down, but don't wrap it around anything.

SUPPLIES

* coat hanger
* paper
* pencil
* markers
* scissors
* hole punch
* tape
* 2 pipe cleaners
* string at least 24 inches long
* 2 chairs with top bars
* index cards that are 2 different colors
* clothespins or large paper clips

WHAT DID THE FISHING POLE SAY TO THE FISH?

Catch you later!

6 Tie each end of the string to the top bar on the back of a different chair. Hang the coat hanger on the string.

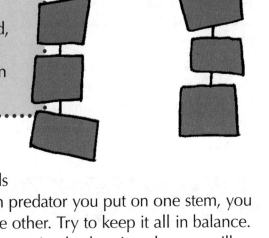

7 On one color index card, draw or write the name of different predators that can live in the habitat you drew. On the other color index card, draw or write the names of different prey animals that can live in the habitat you drew.

8 Use the paper clips or clothespins to attach the cards to the pipe cleaners. For each predator you put on one stem, you must put a prey animal on the other. Try to keep it all in balance. Be careful: If you add too many animals, the pipe cleaners will slip out! This means there are too many animals for your habitat.

TRY THIS! Cut the cards to represent the different sizes of the predators and prey. A mouse would have a small card and coyote would have a big card. How does this change the game?

WILDLIFE FOOD PYRAMID

The first activity in this book encouraged you to take a closer look at the things you eat. Now that you have learned more about predators and prey, make a food pyramid for the wildlife in your area!

1 Open your journal to the page titled "My Food Journal." It is okay if you did not do that activity. You can still do this one.

2 On the back of the double-page spread, make a new chart to record all the animals you see or hear. For 24 hours, keep track of ALL the animals you see, hear, or see signs of, such as spider webs and bird poop on the car. Hint: Try to pick a day with good weather.

Animal	Alive, dead, or sign	How many?	Herbivore, omnivore or carnivore?
Robin	Alive	2	Carnivore (eating worms)

PROJECT!

3 After 24 hours, write the name of each herbivore you saw on a separate green index card. Write the name of each carnivore you saw on a separate red index card. Write the name of each omnivore you saw on a separate yellow index card. Each animal gets its own card! If you saw 10 sparrows, you should make 10 green sparrow cards.

4 Group the cards together by color. Count the number of cards of each color. Make a line of colored cards that has the greatest number. The second largest number of colored cards goes in a line above this. The color that has the least number of cards goes on top. What does this food pyramid tell you about predator-prey relationships in your area?

THINK MORE: Take a photo of this pyramid or use colored pencils and draw it on the page opposite your "Top This!" food pyramid. Compare the two. Do you think these pyramids accurately reflect the natural world around you?

A WARM MEAL

Warm-blooded animals need more food energy than cold-blooded ones to stay alive. A wolf must eat about seven pounds of meat each day to stay healthy. An alligator that weighs about the same amount only needs seven pounds of meat each week to stay healthy! Wolves can live in cold or warm places. Alligators must stay where it is warm.

PROJECT!

KEEP AWAY

SUPPLIES

* plastic food container with lid
* rocks
* scissors
* animal model from Chapter 4
* dowel rod
* clay

Many ranchers and farmers worry that coyotes, wolves, and even eagles prey on their lambs and baby cows. Scientists study ways to keep predators away from farm animals. Can you keep animals away from your area?

1 Fill the plastic container with rocks for your base.

2 Use the scissors to poke a hole in the top and bottom of the animal model. Also poke a hole in the lid of the plastic container.

3 Poke the dowel rod through the hole in the animal model. Make two small balls of clay. Roll each one into a rope. Wrap a rope around the dowel rod on the top and bottom of the model. This will help hold it in place.

4 Place the bottom end of the dowel rod in the weighted plastic container. If the model falls over, move it farther down the dowel rod until it is balanced. Take it outside.

5 Observe the area around your model and record any reactions from other animals.

THINK ABOUT IT: Are there any scarecrows, plastic owls, or other decoys around the area you live? A decoy is used to lure or scare an animal. What are they protecting? Do they work? What changes can you make to the decoy to make it work better?

A

adaptation: a body part or behavior that has developed to do a specific job for an animal or plant.

adapt: the changes a plant or animal makes to survive in new or different conditions.

amphibian: an animal, such as a toad, frog, or salamander, that is born in the water and lives on land.

B

baleen: the tough, flexible material hanging down in some whales' mouths to help trap their food.

C

camouflage: colors or patterns that allow a plant or animal to blend in with its environment.

canine teeth: the longest, strongest, pointiest tooth in mammals, used for stabbing, ripping, and tearing.

carnassial: a square-shaped, sharp-pointed tooth in the middle and back of carnivorous mammal jaws.

carnivore: an animal that eats only other animals, or meat.

carnivorous plant: a plant that traps and eats animals.

cell: the basic unit or part of a living thing. Cells are so small they can be seen only with a microscope. Billions of cells make up an animal or plant.

chemical: a substance that has certain features that can react with other substances.

colorblind: unable to see color.

D

defense: protection from attack.

diurnal: active during the day.

downwind: to have an object between you and the direction of the wind.

E

echolocation: to find an object by making sounds, then hearing how the sounds bounce back to your ears.

ecologist: a scientist who studies plants and animals and their habitat.

ecosystem: a community of plants and animals living in an area, relying on each other to survive.

endangered: a plant or animal with a very low population that is at risk of disappearing entirely.

energy: the ability or power to do things, to work.

evade: to escape or avoid getting caught.

evolution: changing gradually during many years.

G

generation: a group born and living at about the same time.

H

habitat: the natural area where a plant or animal lives.

herbivore: an animal that eats only plants.

I

immune: able to resist a disease or a toxin.

incisor: a front, chisel-shaped tooth in mammals, used for cutting.

inherit: to acquire something from a parent or grandparent.

L

lure: an object, smell, or sound that attracts animals.

M

mammal: an animal such as a human, dog, or cat. Mammals are born live, feed milk to their young, and usually have hair or fur covering most of their skin.

minerals: nutrients found in rocks and soil that keep plants and animals healthy and growing. Salt and nitrogen are two minerals.

molar: a flattened, square-shaped tooth at the back of the jaw in mammals, used for chewing or grinding.

musk: a strong-smelling odor from the musk deer or another animal.

N

nocturnal: to be active at night.

nutrients: the substances found in food that a plant or animal needs to live and grow.

O

odor: the scent of something.

omnivore: an animal that eats plants and other animals.

organ: a part of the body with a specific job. Organs include your heart, lungs, and skin.

organism: a living thing, such as a plant or animal.

P

parasite: a plant or animal that feeds on another plant or animal without directly killing it.

photosynthesis: the process plants use to convert the sun's energy into food.

predator: an animal or plant that kills and eats another animal.

premolar: a somewhat flat, square-shaped tooth near the middle of the jaw in mammals, used for chewing or grinding.

prey: an animal that is hunted by a predator.

R

reptile: an animal covered with scales that crawls on its belly or on short legs. A snake, turtle, lizard, and alligator are all reptiles.

S

scavenger: an animal that feeds on animals that are already dead.

stalk: to quietly follow prey.

survive: to stay alive.

T

taste buds: a cluster of nerve endings that senses taste.

tool: an object that helps get a job done.

toxin: a poison that can cause sickness or death.

V

venom: a poison made by some animals that is injected into other animals to cause pain or death.

METRIC CONVERSIONS

Use this chart to find the metric equivalents to the English measurements in this book. If you need to know a half measurement, divide by two. If you need to know twice the measurement, multiply by two. How do you find a quarter measurement? How do you find three times the measurement?

English	Metric
1 inch	2.5 centimeters
1 foot	30.5 centimeters
1 yard	0.9 meter
1 mile	1.6 kilometers
1 pound	0.5 kilogram
1 teaspoon	5 milliliters
1 tablespoon	15 milliliters
1 cup	237 milliliters

BOOKS

Tooth & Claw: The Wild World of Big Predators.
Arnosky, Jim. Sterling, 2014

Bubble Homes and Fish Farts. Bayrock, Fiona.
Charlesbridge, 2009

Animal Tongues. Cusick, Dawn.
Early Light, 2009

Where's Waldo. Handford, Martin.
Candlewick, 2012

Eyewitness: Animal. Jackson, Tom.
Dorling Kindersley, 2012

*You Wouldn't Want to Be a Mammoth Hunter! Dangerous Beasts
You'd Rather Not Encounter.* Malam, John. Franklin Watts, 2004

The Queen's Shadow: A Story About How Animals See.
Young, Cybéle. Kids Can Press, 2015

VIDEOS

4 Incredible Photosynthetic Animals
umich.uloop.com/news/view.php/77109/4-incredible-photosynthetic-animals

How Animals See the World
youtube.com/watch?v=6hYaT4gvjNc

Daniel Kish uses ears to see
cnn.com/2011/11/09/tech/innovation/daniel-kish-poptech-echolocation

Where's Waldo?
whereswaldo.com/index.html#home

Animal Protection Adaptations

slideshare.net/MMoiraWhitehouse/animal-protection-adapations-teach

QR CODE GLOSSARY

Page 2: umich.uloop.com/news/view.php/77109/4-incredible-photosynthetic-animals

Page 4: phenomena.nationalgeographic.com/2015/07/02/single-celled-creature-has-eye-made-of-domesticated-microbes

Page 7: crossfitimpulse.com/nutritional-first-steps

Page 17: factmonster.com/ipka/A0769023.html

Page 26: video.nationalgeographic.com/video/ngexpeditions/humpback-bubble-net

Page 29: photography.nationalgeographic.com/photography/photos/patterns-nature-spider-webs/australia-spider-web.html

Page 31: allaboutbirds.org/guide/Black-capped_Chickadee/sounds

Page 36: youtube.com/watch?v=FJ_RA_T5bgg

Page 50: yellowstonepark.com/wolf-reintroduction-changes-ecosystem

Page 59: youtube.com/watch?v=YPoDbi8yXJM

Page 64: phenomena.nationalgeographic.com/2013/02/28/tongue-eating-fish-parasites-never-cease-to-amaze

Page 67: bugfacts.net

Page 69: adventurescience.org/roadkill.html

ESSENTIAL QUESTIONS

Introduction: How does where you live affect what you eat?

Chapter 1: Sight, smell, hearing, touch, and taste are your five senses. Which sense do many humans rely on the most?

Chapter 2: What tools set humans apart from other predators?

Chapter 3: How would you get food in your mouth if you didn't have hands?

Chapter 4: What are some strategies you use to stay safe at home and at school?

Chapter 5: If mosquitoes disappeared, what effect could that have on other animals and the ecosystem?

Chapter 6: How do humans change the balance between predators and prey?